The title poem of *The Mills of the Kavanaughs* is a dramatic narrative of some 600 lines. The setting is "a village a little north of Bath, Maine," and most of the poem is Anne Kavanaugh's reverie, addressed to her dead husband.

In addition to the title poem, Mr. Lowell includes five long poems—"Falling Asleep Over the Aeneid," "Thanksgiving's Over," "Mother Marie Therese," "David and Bathsheba in the Public Garden," and "Her Dead Brother"—and an "imitation after Werfel" entitled "The Fat Man in the Mirror."

THE MILLS OF THE KAVANAUGHS

Other Books by Robert Lowell

LORD WEARY'S CASTLE • LAND OF UNLIKENESS

THE MILLS OF THE KAVANAUGHS

ROBERT LOWELL

HARCOURT, BRACE & WORLD, INC. : NEW YORK

Drawing on title page by Francis Parker

FOR MY MOTHER,
AND IN MEMORY OF MY FATHER

These poems have appeared in *The Kenyon Review*, *The Nation*, *Poetry* and *Partisan Review* and, excepting the title poem, in *Poems: 1938-1949*, published by Messrs. Faber and Faber, London. "The Fat Man in the Mirror" is not a translation but an imitation.

Contents

The Mills of the Kavanaughs

"Ah, love let us be true
To one another! for the world, which seems
To lie before us like a land of dreams . . ."
[DOVER BEACH]

"Morals are the memory of success that no longer
succeeds." [IN THE AMERICAN GRAIN]

An afternoon in the fall of 1943; a village a little north of Bath, Maine. Anne Kavanaugh is sitting in her garden playing solitaire. She pretends that the Bible she has placed in the chair opposite her is her opponent. At one end of the garden is the grave of her husband, Harry Kavanaugh, a naval officer who was retired after Pearl Harbor. The Kavanaughs are a Catholic family that came to Maine in the 17th century. Their house is called *Kavanaugh*; it is on a hill, and at its foot, there is a mill pond, and by it a marble statue of Persephone, the goddess who became a queen by becoming queen of the dead. The Abnakis, or Penobscots, are almost extinct Maine Indians, who were originally converted by the French. Anne comes of a poor family. She was adopted by the Kavanaughs many years before she married. Most of the poem is a revery of her childhood and marriage, and is addressed to her dead husband.

THE Douay Bible on the garden chair
  Facing the lady playing solitaire
In blue-jeans and a sealskin toque from Bath
Is *Sol*, her dummy. There's a sort of path
Or rut of weeds that serpents down a hill
And graveyard to a ruined burlap mill;
There, a maternal nineteenth century
Italian statue of Persephone
Still beckons to a mob of Bacchanals
To plunge like dogs or athletes through the falls,
And fetch her the stone garland she will hurl.
The lady drops her cards. She kneels to furl
Her husband's flag, and thinks his mound and stone
Are like a buried bed. "This is the throne
They must have willed us. Harry, not a thing
Was missing: we were children of a king.

"Our people had kept up their herring weirs,
Their rum and logging grants two hundred years,
When Cousin Franklin Pierce was President—
Almost three hundred, Harry, when you sent
His signed engraving sailing on your kite
Above the gable, where your mother's light,
A daylight bulb in tortoise talons, pipped
The bull-mad june-bugs on the manuscript
That she was typing to redeem our mills
From Harding's taxes, and we lost our means
Of drawing pulp and water from those hills
Above the Saco, where our tenants drilled
Abnaki partisans for Charles the First,
And seated our Republicans, while Hearst
And yellow paper fed the moose that swilled
Our spawning ponds for weeds like spinach greens.

"Love, is it trespassing to call them ours?
They are now. Once I trespassed—picking flowers
For keepsakes of my journey, once I bent
Above your well, where lawn and battlement
Were trembling, yet without a flaw to mar
Their sweet surrender. Ripples seemed to star
My face, the rocks, the bottom of the well;
My heart, pursued by all its plunder, fell,
And I was tossing petals from my lair
Of copper leaves above your mother's chair.
Alone in that *verboten*, how I mocked
Her erudition, while she read and rocked.
And how I queened it, when she let me lop
At pigeons with my lilliputian crop,
And pester squirrels from that beech tree's bole
Colored with bunting like a barber's pole."

The lady sees the statues in the pool.
She dreams and thinks, "My husband was a fool
To run out from the Navy when disgrace
Still wanted zeal to look him in the face."
She wonders why her fancy makes her look
Across the table, where the open Book
Forgets the ease and honor of its shelf
To tell her that her gambling with herself
Is love of self. She pauses, drops the deck,
And feels her husband's fingers touch her neck.
She thinks of Daphne—Daphne could outrun
The birds, and saw her swiftness tire the sun,
And yet, perhaps, saw nothing to admire
Beneath Apollo, when his crackling fire
Stood rooted, half unwilling to undo
Her laurel branches dropping from the blue.

4

The leaves, sun's yellow, listen, Love, they fall.
She hears her husband, and she tries to call
Him, then remembers. Burning stubble roars
About the garden. Columns fill the life
Insurance calendar on which she scores.
The lady laughs. She shakes her parasol.
The table rattles, and she chews her pearled,
Once telescopic pencil, till its knife
Snaps open. *"Sol,"* she whispers, laughing, *"Sol,*
If you will help me, I will win the world."
Her husband's thumbnail scratches on her comb.
A boy is pointing at the sun. He cries:
O dandelion, wish my wish, be true,
And blows the callow pollen in her eyes.
"Harry," she whispers, "we are far from home—
A boy and girl a-Maying in the blue

"Of March or April. We are tumbling through
The chalk-pits to our rural demigod,
Old skull-and-horns, the bullock Father slew,
There on the sky-line. Let the offal sod
Our fields with Ceres. Here is piety;
Ceres is here replenished to the full—
Green the clairvoyance of her deity,
Although the landscape's like a bullock's skull . . .
Things held together once," she thinks. "But where?
Not for the life of me! How can I see
Things as they are, my Love, while April steals
Through bog and chalk-pit, till these boulders bear
Persephone—illusory, perhaps,
Yet her renewal, no illusion, for this air
Is orgied, Harry, and your setter yaps
About the goddess, while it nips her heels."

5

The setter worries through the coils of brush
And steaming bramble, and the children rush
Hurrahing, where no marsh or scrubby field
Or sorry clump of virgin pine will yield
A moment's covert to the half-extinct
And pileated bird they trail with linked
Fingers and little burlap sacks of salt.
The bird, a wise old uncle, knows what fault
Or whimsy guides the children when they halt
For sling-stones. Too distinguished to exalt,
It drops and cruises, while the children vault
The trifling mill-stream, where it used to kill
The sandsnakes in the flotsam with its bill;
Its stoned red-tufted shadow skims the pond;
Now it is lifting, now it clears the mill,
And, tired with child's-play, sails beyond beyond.

The children splash and paddle. Then, hand in hand,
They duck for turtles. Where she cannot stand,
The whirlpool sucks her. She has set her teeth
Into his thumb. She wrestles underneath
The sea-green smother; stunned, unstrung and torn
Into a thousand globules by that horn
Or whorl of river, she has burst apart
Like churning water on her husband's heart—
A horny thumbnail! Then they lie beside
The marble goddess. "Look, the stony-eyed
Persephone has mouldered like a leaf!"
The children whisper. Old and pedestalled,
Where rock-pools used to echo when she called
Demeter—sheathed in Lincoln green, a sheaf—
The statue of Persephone regards
The river, while it moils a hundred yards

Below her garland. Here, they used to build
A fire to broil their trout. A beer can filled
With fishskins marks the dingle where they died.
They whisper, "Touch her. If her foot should slide
A little earthward, Styx will hold her down
Nella miseria, smashed to plaster, balled
Into the whirlpool's boil." Here bubbles filled
Their basin, and the children splashed. They died
In Adam, while the grass snake slid appalled
To summer, while Jehovah's grass-green lyre
Was rustling all about them in the leaves
That gurgled by them turning upside down;
The time of marriage!—worming on all fours
Up slag and deadfall, while the torrent pours
Down, down, down, down—and she, a crested bird,
Or rainbow, hovers, lest the thunder-word

Deluge her playmate in Jehovah's beard
Of waterfalls. She listens to his feared
Footsteps, no longer muffled by the green
Torrent, that serpents up and down between
Them, while she sprints along the shelf.
Her toes curl. "I am married to myself,"
She hears him shout, and answers, "All for us."
And *ah, ah, ah* echoes the cavernous
Cascading froth's crescendo: *Stammerer,*
You cannot answer, Child, you cannot answer.
She wades. The boy, too small to follow her,
Calls out in anger, and three times her answer
Struggles to tell him, but her bubbles star
The cheerful surface idly. She is part
Of the down-under beating like her heart.
Although the voice is near her, it sounds far.

"The world hushed. Dying in your arms, I heard
The mowers moving through that golden-eared
Avernal ambush, and I seemed to hear
The harvesters, who rose to volunteer
As escorts for Persephone's deferred
Renewal of the earth, so vainly feared;
And all their voices, light as feathers, sighed
Unwelcome to that violated bride,
Uncertain even of her hold on hell,
Who curbed her horses, as if serpent-stung,
While shadows massed in earnest to rebel.
Weary and glorious, once, when time was young,
She ran from Hades. All Avernus burned.
Black horse and chariot thundered at her heel.
She, fleeting earthward, nothing seemed to steal,
But the fruition that her hell had earned.

"On days of Obligation, if our farm
Stockaded by wild cherries, and the spruce
My father hacked like weeds to keep us warm
Through summer, if it crossed your path; what use
Was it? His thirteen children and his goat,
Those cook-stove heated clapboards, where we slept
In relays, beaver dams of cans, a moat
Our cesspool drained on—if on that, he kept
A second woman twenty farms up road;
What use was it? The air we breathed he owed
The poor-box. Is it throwing money down
A well to help the poor? They die. They glitter
Like a cathedral—whiskey, tears and tapers.
He died. Your mother came and signed my papers.
She plucked me like a kitten from that litter,
And charged my board and lodging to the town.

"Your house, can you forget it? Or its *school*,
Where Bowdoin students taught us cowboy pool—
Brother and sister! How Abnakis, screened
In bleeding sumac, scared us, when they leaned
Against us—pocked and warlocked—to pursue
Their weaponed shadows raiding through the dew
Of twilight after crickets? How we spiked
Our bows with pears for flinging? When we hiked
Homeward, you winged our falcon with a rock—
Fumbling for the tail-feathers of a cock,
Blue-blooded, gluttonous, it swallowed blood,
While mother fetched its parrot perch and hood,
And set it by the daub of Kavanaugh,
Sheriff for Lincoln County and the King,
Whose old two-handed eighteenth century saw
Hung like a whale's jaw lashed with bits of string.

"The blazings of the woodsman left a track
Straight as an arrow to the blacksmith's shack
Where I was born. There, just a month before
Our marriage, I can see you: we had dressed
Ourselves in holly, and you cut your crest,
A stump and green shoots on my father's door,
And swore our marriage would renew the cleft
Forests and skulls of the Abnakis left
Like saurian footprints by the lumber lord,
Who broke their virgin greenness cord by cord
To build his clearing. Once his axe was law
And culture, but this house in its decline
Forgets how tender green shoots used to spring
From the decaying stump—Red Kavanaugh
Who built it, and inscribed its Latin line:
Cut down we flourish, on his signet ring.

"And there was greenwood spitting on the fire-dogs,
That looked like Hessians. It was June, and Maine
Smouldered to greenness, and the perching frogs
Chirred to the greener sizzle of a rain
That freshened juniper and Wilson's thrush
Before the Revolution. We were hot,
And climbed the Portland wagon-road to push
Past vineyards to the *praying niggers'* lot.
There, the Abnakis, christened by the French,
Chanted our *Miserere*. Love, how wild,
Their fragrance! Grouse were pecking on their trench—
Red Kavanaugh's, who burned and buried child
And squaw and elder in their river bed,
A pine-tree shilling a scalp; yes, scalped their king
In the dead drop—and both already dead,
Drowned in the dazzling staidness of our spring.

"Marriage by drowning! Soon enough our own,"
She whispers, laughing. "Though they left no stone
Unturned to stop us, soon the maids in red
Were singing Cinderella at our mass;
They called me Cinderella, but I said:
'Prince Charming is my shadow in the glass.'"
The lady stacks her cards. She laughs and scores.
She dreams. Her husband holds his mansion doors
Open. He helps the bridesmaids, stoops to tie
Her roses. "Anne," he teases, "Anne, my whole
House is your serf. The squirrel in its hole
Who hears your patter, Anne, and sinks its eye-
Teeth, bigger than a human's, in its treasure
Of rotten shells, is wiser far than I
Who have forsaken all my learning's leisure
To be your man and husband—God knows why!"

"God knows," she wonders, "when I watched you sail
From Boston Harbor on the *Arkansas*
For the Pacific, I was glad. No mail
Until December. You returned. I saw
Your horses pulling up the hill, and heard
You crying like a white, bewildered bird
The sea rejected. You were on the floor,
And clowning like a boy. You grimaced, bared
Your chest, and bellowed, 'Listen, undeclared
War seems to . . . static . . . the United States
And Honolulu are at war. War, War!
Pearl Harbor's burning!' But I knew you cared
Little, and that was why you turned to creak
The rusty hinges of the oven door.
You creaked and puttered, till I thought our plates
Of numbered birds would smash their frames, and shriek.

"The horses stumbled, and we had to stop.
The mountain soared. Its top, the Widow's Walk,
A mile above us, balanced on a drop,
Where dryfall after dryfall crashed to chalk.
The roots were charcoal. Standing shells of stocks
At each meander marched to block our climb
Along a snake-trail weighted down with rocks.
This was Avernus. There, about this time,
Demeter's daughter first reviewed the dead—
Most doomed and pompous, while the maples shed
Their martyr's rubric, and a torrent stood
Stock-still, reflecting; and she heard the bell,
Then lifted on a crossing wind, alarm
The river parish by her mother's farm—
There, hearing how she'd come to little good,
She took a husband to dispirit hell."

She thinks of how she watched her husband drive
To meetings with Macaulay's life of Clive
Tucked in a pocket—there, unshaven, white,
And mumbling to himself, he would recite
The verses on Lucretia from the *Lay
Of Ancient Rome*, and ape her Roman way
Of falling from dishonor on a sword;
And yet she'd thought her kindness had restored
Pearl Harbor's shell-shock, thought he would enjoy . . .
As if God's touch, as if Jehovah's joy,
Allowed him to resume the wearisome
Renown of merely living, when he'd come,
Like Atlas with the world about his ears,
To tell her nothing. Once again she hears
Her husband's stubborn laugh. A pair of boulder
Gray squirrels romp like kittens on his shoulder.

Then it was Christmas. "Harry's mine for good,"
She'd shouted, running down the stairs to find
Him stumbling for his little strip of wood
To stir the bowl. She sees the flurries blind
The barren Christmas greens, as winter dusks
The double window, and she hears the slow
Treck of the Magi hoofing cotton snow
Behind their snow-shoes on the golden husks
Of birdseed cast like breadcrumbs for their three
Gold-dusty camels by the Christmas tree,
A withered creeping hemlock in a cup;
Its star of hope and only ornament,
A silver dollar. He turned the burners up,
And stirred the stoup of glüg—a quart of grain,
Two quarts of claret, every condiment,
Berry and nut and rind and herb in Maine!

"You went to bed, Love, finished—through, through, through.
Hoping to find you useless, dead asleep,
I stole to bed beside you, after two
As usual. Had you drugged yourself to keep
Your peace? I think so. If our bodies met,
You'd flinch, and flounder on your face. I heard
The snowplow banging; its eye-headlights set
On mine—a clowning dragon—so absurd,
Its thirty gangling feet of angled lights,
Red, blue and orange. Having broken loose
From Ringling Brothers, it had lost the use
Of sense, Love, and was worming days and nights
To hole up *some*where. Then I slept. I found
That I was stalking in my moccasins
Below the mill-fall, where our cave begins
To shake its head, a green Medusa, crowned

With juniper. A dragon writhed around
A knob above you, and its triple tails
Fanned at your face. Furlongs of glaucous scales
Wallowed to splatter the reproachful hound
Eyes of the gorgon on the monstrous targe,
Plated with hammered-down tobacco tins,
You pushed and parried at the water's charge.
Your blue and orange broadsword lopped its fins
And roaring . . . I was back in bed. The day
Was graying on us. So that you could keep
An eye upon them, Harry, sword and shield
Loomed from your shoebag. "I will have to yield
You to the dragon, if you fall asleep."
You pulled my nightgown. "Maiden, they have belled
The dragon's tail. The dragon's on its way
To woo you." Then I slept. Your fingers held. . . .

"You *held* me! 'Please, Love, let your elbows . . . quick,
Quick it!' I shook you, 'can't you see how sick
This playing . . . take me; Harry's driving back.
Take me!' 'Who am I?' 'You are you; not black
Like Harry; you're a boy. Look out, his car's
White eyes are at the window. Boy, your chin
Is bristling. You have gored me black and blue.
I am all prickle-tickle like the stars;
I am a sleepy-foot, a dogfish skin
Rubbed backwards, wrongways; you have made my hide
Split snakey, Bad one—*one!*' Then I was wide
Awake, and turning over. 'Who, who, who?'
You asked me, 'tell me who.' Then everything
Was roaring, Harry. Harry, I could feel
Nothing—it was so black—except your seal,
The stump with green shoots on your signet ring.

"I couldn't tell you; but you shook the bed,
And struck me, Harry. 'I will shake you dead
As earth,' you chattered, 'you, you, you, you, you. . . .
Who are you keeping, Anne?' you mocked me, 'Anne,
You want yourself.' I gagged, and then I ran.
My maid was knocking. Snow was chasing through
The open window. 'Harry, I am glad
You tried to kill me; it is out, you know;
I'll shout it from the housetops of the Mills;
I'll tell you, so remember, you are mad;
I'll tell them, listen Harry: husband kills
His wife for dreaming. You must help. No, no!
I've always loved you; I am just a girl;
You mustn't choke me!' Then I thought the beams
Were falling on us. Things began to whirl.
'Harry, we're not accountable for dreams.'

14

"Spread-eagled backward on your backless chair,
Inhaling the regardless, whirling air,
Rustling about you from the oven jets,
Sparkling and crackling on the cigarettes
Still burning in the saucer, where you'd tossed
Almost a carton, Love, before you lost
All sense of caring, and I saw your eyes
Looking in wonder at your bloody hand—
And like an angler wading out from land,
Who feels the bottom shelving, while he sees
His nibbled bobber twitch the dragonflies:
You watched your hand withdrawing by degrees—
Enthralled and fearful—till it stopped beneath
Your collar, and you felt your being drip
Blue-purple with a joy that made your teeth
Grin all to-whichways through your lower lip.

"I must have fainted. Harry, where I sank,
The gulls were yelping and a river stank,
And I was seated in a wicker chair
Beside a tub of crabs. And you were there
Above me and I held a jelly-roll
And read the comics, while you stood to pole
Our dory with a pitchfork to the pier.
You shout directions, but I cannot steer
Because the boat stops, and the spilling tub
Bubbles with torment, as you trip and lance
Your finger at a crab. It strikes. You rub
It inch-meal to a bilge of shell. You dance
Child-crazy over tub and gunnel, grasping
Your pitchfork like a trident, poised to stab
The greasy eel-grass clasping and unclasping
The jellied iridescence of the crab.

"Then yellow water, and the summer's drought
Boiled on its surface underneath our grounds'
Disordered towzle. *Wish my, wish my, wish*,
Said the dry-flies snapping past my ears to whip
Those dead-horse waters, faster than a fish
Could follow—longer too. I gasped. My mouth
Was open, and I seemed to mime your hound's
Terrified panting; and our trimming ship
Was shipping water . . . I was staring at
Our drifting oars. The moon was floating—flat
As the old world of maps. I thought, 'I'll stay.
Harry,' I whispered, 'hurry, I will pray
So truly; hurry! God, you must, you must
Hurry, for Death, carousing like a king
On nothing but his lands, will take your ring
To bind me, and possess me to the dust.'

"Then life went on; you lived, or lived at least
To baby-smile into the brutal gray
Daylight each morning, and your sofa lay
Beside the window, and you watched the east
Wind romping, till it swept the sullen blue
Bluster of April in the mouth of May,
The month of mating. Yellow warblers flew
About the ivied window, calling you.
You smiled. Then your eyes wandered to alight
As aliens on your charts of black and white
New England birds: the kinds, once memorized
By number, now no longer recognized,
Were numbers, numbers! 'What's the twenty-eight,
The twenty-eight, the twenty-eight—O wait:
A cardinal bird, a scarlet tanager,
The redbird that I used to whittle her.'

"You lived. Your rocker creaked, as you declined.
To the ungarnished ruin of your mind
Came the persona of the murderous Saul
In dirty armor, followed by a boy,
Who twanged a jew's-harp. Stumbling on one leg,
You speared our quaking shadows to the wall.
'Where is my harper? Music! Must I beg
For music?' Then you sucked your thumb for joy,
And baby-smiled through strings of orange juice.
'Where are you, Anne? A harper for the King.'
When the phantasmagoria left, you wept
For their return. Ah Harry, what's the use
Of lying? I called the doctor while you slept.
'Now it's as if he'd never lived,' I thought;
'As if I'd never, never anything.'
I felt the stump and green shoots at my throat.

" 'Sleep, sleep,' I hushed you. 'Sleep. You must abide
The lamentations of the nuptial mass—
Then you are rising. Then you are alive;
The bridesmaids scatter daisies, and the bride,
A daisy choired by daisies, sings: "My life
Is like a horn of plenty gone to grass,
Or like the yellow bee-queen in her hive."
She whispers, "Who is this, and who is this?
His eyes are coals. His breath is myrrh; his kiss,
The consummation of the silvered glass.
His lightning slivers through me like a knife." '
The door is open, but I hope to pass
Unheard. Your male-attendant tries to feed
You. I can hear him talking (O for keeps!)
'Mother of Jesus, had her while she sleeps;
She took him for the other guy, she'd . . .' *She'd!*"

Then summer followed: children rollerskate
And fight with hockey sticks about a crate
Of cannon crackers. They have mined the road.
Someone is shouting. Tufts of grass explode.
Somewhere a child is dancing in his grease
And war-paint. "Mees," he shouts, "town ring! Mees, Mees,
Town ring. Lieutenant Kavanaugh eeth dead."
She sees the body sitting up in bed
Before the window. "You must bury me
As if you gloried in my liberty.
I died," it seems to tell her, "while July,
The month of freedom, tigerstriped the sky
With bombs and rockets." How will she disown
The leisured condescension of his frown
That still refuses, while she moves about
The body, saying, "Blow the candle out."

"But it's so dull," she whispers, "it's so dull,
This autumn, Harry, from the line-storm lull
Through Hallows', playing Patience to defeat
Poor *Sol.* Pearl Harbor's whole Pacific fleet
Has sea-room in my mind. Here, Peace, the Pearl
Hawaiians dive for . . . I am just a girl,
Just one man's not the fleet's." She stands, then sits
And makes a card-house; it's as if her wits
Were overseas. The cards are Kavanaughs,
Or sinister, bewildered effigies
Of kings and queens. Another game begins;
Shuffling so badly that she always wins,
She dreams her luck has brought her husband home.
"Harry," she whispers, "listen, the applause
Is rising for you. Gods of ancient Rome
Rise from the mill-pond on their marble knees.

"They watch like water-polo players—their eyes,
Stars of a recognition, no disguise
Or veil will hinder, now that they have found
Me their Persephone, gone underground
Into myself to supplicate the throne
And horn of Hades to restore that stone,
Imperial garland, once the living flower,
Now stone—Harvest, my mother's, only dower
To the dark monarch, and the futile dead
In Hades, where I lost my maidenhead.
Horns of the moon, they chant, *our Goddess.*" Then
She wakes. She stacks her cards, and once again
She rambles down the weedy path, past hill
And graveyard to the ruined burlap mill.
She lifts a pail. She pushes on an oar.
Her metal boat is moving from the shore.

The heron warps its neck, a broken pick,
To study its reflection on the scales,
Or knife-bright shards of water lilies, quick
In the dead autumn water with their snails
And water lice. Her ballet glasses hold
Him twisted by a fist of spruce, as dry
As flint and steel. She thinks: "The bird is old,
A cousin to all scholars; that is why
He will abet my thoughts of Kavanaugh,
Who gave the Mills its lumberyard and weir
In eighteen hundred, when our farmers saw
John Adams bring their Romish church a bell,
Cast—so the records claim—by Paul Revere.
The sticks of *Kavanaugh* are buried here—
Many of them, too many, Love, to tell—
Faithful to where their virgin forest fell.

And now the mussed blue-bottles bead her float:
Bringers of luck. Of luck? At worst, a rest
From counting blisters on her metal boat,
That spins and staggers. North and south and west:
A scene, perhaps, of Fragonard—her park,
Whose planted poplars scatter penny-leaves,
White underneath, like mussels to the dark
Chop of the shallows. Extirpation grieves
The sunken martyred laughter of the loon,
Where Harry's mother bathed in navy-blue
Stockings and skirts. But now, the afternoon
Is sullen, it is all that she can do
To lift the anchor. She can hardly row
Against these whitecaps—surely never lulled
For man and woman. Washing to and fro,
The floorboards bruise the lilies that she pulled.

"Even in August it was autumn—all
A pond could harbor." Now her matches fall
In dozens by her bobber to expire
As target-circles on the mirrored fire-
Escapes of *Kavanaugh*. She sees they hold
Her mirror to her—just a little cold;
A ground hog's looking glass. "The day is sharp
And short, Love, and its sun is like this carp,
Or goldfish, almost twenty inches long,
Panting, a weak old dog, below a prong
Of deadwood fallen from my copper beech;
The settling leaves embower its warmth. They reach
For my reflection, but it glides through shoal
Aground, to where the squirrel held its roots
And freehold, Love, unsliding, when our boots
Pattered—a life ago once—on its hole.

"I think we row together, for the stern
Jumps from my weaker stroke, and down the cove
Our house is floating, and the windows burn,
As if its underpinnings fed the stove.
Her window's open; look, she waits for us,
And types, until the clattering tin bell
Upon her room-large table tolls for us.
Listen, your mother's asking, *is it well?*
Yes, very well. He died outside the church
Like Harry Tudor. Now we near the sluice
And burial ground above the burlap mill;
I see you swing a string of yellow perch
About your head to fan off gnats that mill
And wail, as your disheartened shadow tries
The buried bedstead, where your body lies—
Time out of mind—a failing stand of spruce.

"God knows!" she marvels. "Harry, *Kavanaugh*
Was lightly given. Soon enough we saw
Death like the Bourbon after Waterloo,
Who learning and forgetting nothing, knew
Nothing but ruin. Why must we mistrust
Ourselves with Death who takes the world on trust?
Although God's brother, and himself a god,
Death whipped his horses through the startled sod;
For neither conscience nor omniscience warned
Him from his folly, when the virgin scorned
His courtship, and the quaking earth revealed
Death's desperation to the Thracian field.
And yet we think the virgin took no harm:
She gave herself because her blood was warm—
And for no other reason, Love, I gave
Whatever brought me gladness to the grave."

Falling Asleep over the Aeneid

An old man in Concord forgets to go to morning service. He falls asleep, while reading Vergil, and dreams that he is Aeneas at the funeral of Pallas, an Italian prince.

THE sun is blue and scarlet on my page,
   And *yuck-a, yuck-a, yuck-a, yuck-a,* rage
The yellowhammers mating. Yellow fire
Blankets the captives dancing on their pyre,
And the scorched lictor screams and drops his rod.
Trojans are singing to their drunken God,
Ares. Their helmets catch on fire. Their files
Clank by the body of my comrade—miles
Of filings! Now the scythe-wheeled chariot rolls
Before their lances long as vaulting poles,
And I stand up and heil the thousand men,
Who carry Pallas to the bird-priest. Then
The bird-priest groans, and as his birds foretold,
I greet the body, lip to lip. I hold
The sword that Dido used. It tries to speak,
A bird with Dido's sworded breast. Its beak
Clangs and ejaculates the Punic word
I hear the bird-priest chirping like a bird.
I groan a little. "Who am I, and why?"
It asks, a boy's face, though its arrow-eye
Is working from its socket. "Brother, try,
O Child of Aphrodite, try to die:
To die is life." His harlots hang his bed
With feathers of his long-tailed birds. His head
Is yawning like a person. The plumes blow;
The beard and eyebrows ruffle. Face of snow,
You are the flower that country girls have caught,
A wild bee-pillaged honey-suckle brought
To the returning bridegroom—the design
Has not yet left it, and the petals shine;

The earth, its mother, has, at last, no help:
It is itself. The broken-winded yelp
Of my Phoenician hounds, that fills the brush
With snapping twigs and flying, cannot flush
The ghost of Pallas. But I take his pall,
Stiff with its gold and purple, and recall
How Dido hugged it to her, while she toiled,
Laughing—her golden threads, a serpent coiled
In cypress. Now I lay it like a sheet;
It clinks and settles down upon his feet,
The careless yellow hair that seemed to burn
Beforehand. Left foot, right foot—as they turn,
More pyres are rising: armored horses, bronze,
And gagged Italians, who must file by ones
Across the bitter river, when my thumb
Tightens into their wind-pipes. The beaks drum;
Their headman's cow-horned death's-head bites its tongue,
And stiffens, as it eyes the hero slung
Inside his feathered hammock on the crossed
Staves of the eagles that we winged. Our cost
Is nothing to the lovers, whoring Mars
And Venus, father's lover. Now his car's
Plumage is ready, and my marshals fetch
His squire, Acoetes, white with age, to hitch
Aethon, the hero's charger, and its ears
Prick, and it steps and steps, and stately tears
Lather its teeth; and then the harlots bring
The hero's charms and baton—but the King,
Vain-glorious Turnus, carried off the rest.
"I was myself, but Ares thought it best
The way it happened." At the end of time,
He sets his spear, as my descendants climb

The knees of Father Time, his beard of scalps,
His scythe, the arc of steel that crowns the Alps.
The elephants of Carthage hold those snows,
Turms of Numidian horse unsling their bows,
The flaming turkey-feathered arrows swarm
Beyond the Alps. "Pallas," I raise my arm
And shout, "Brother, eternal health. Farewell
Forever." Church is over, and its bell
Frightens the yellowhammers, as I wake
And watch the whitecaps wrinkle up the lake.
Mother's great-aunt, who died when I was eight,
Stands by our parlor sabre. "Boy, it's late.
Vergil must keep the Sabbath." Eighty years!
It all comes back. My Uncle Charles appears.
Blue-capped and bird-like. Phillips Brooks and Grant
Are frowning at his coffin, and my aunt,
Hearing his colored volunteers parade
Through Concord, laughs, and tells her English maid
To clip his yellow nostril hairs, and fold
His colors on him. . . . It is I. I hold
His sword to keep from falling, for the dust
On the stuffed birds is breathless, for the bust
Of young Augustus weighs on Vergil's shelf:
It scowls into my glasses at itself.

Her Dead Brother

I

THE Lion of St. Mark's upon the glass
    Shield in my window reddens, as the night
Enchants the swinging dories to its terrors,
And dulls your distant wind-stung eyes; alas,
Your portrait, coiled in German-silver hawsers, mirrors
The sunset as a dragon. Enough light
Remains to see you through your varnish. Giving
Your life has brought you closer to your friends;
Yes, it has brought you home. All's well that ends:
Achilles dead is greater than the living;

My mind holds you as I would have you live,
A wintering dragon. Summer was too short
When we went picnicking with telescopes
And crocking leather handbooks to that fort
Above the lank and heroned Sheepscot, where its slopes
Are clutched by hemlocks—spotting birds. I give
You back that idyll, Brother. Was it more?
Remember riding, scotching with your spur
That four-foot milk-snake in a juniper?
Father shellacked it to the ice-house door.

Then you were grown; I left you on your own.
We will forget that August twenty-third,
When Mother motored with the maids to Stowe,
And the pale summer shades were drawn—so low
No one could see us; no, nor catch your hissing word,
As false as Cressid! Let our deaths atone:
The fingers on your sword-knot are alive,
And Hope, that fouls my brightness with its grace,
Will anchor in the narrows of your face.
My husband's Packard crunches up the drive.

II

(THREE MONTHS LATER)

The ice is out: the tidal current swims
Its blocks against the launches as they pitch
Under the cruisers of my Brother's fleet.
The gas, uncoiling from my oven burners, dims
The face above this bottled *Water Witch*,
The knockabout my Brother fouled and left to eat
Its heart out by the Boston Light. My Brother,
I've saved you in the ice-house of my mind—
The ice is out. . . . Our fingers lock behind
The tiller. We are heeling in the smother,

Our sails, balloon and leg-o'mutton, tell
The colors of the rainbow; but they flap,
As the wind fails, and cannot fetch the bell. . . .
His stick is tapping on the millwheel-step,
He lights a match, another and another—
The Lord is dark, and holy is His name;
By my own hands, into His hands! My burners
Sing like a kettle, and its nickel mirrors
Your squadron by the Stygian Landing. Brother,
The harbor! The torpedoed cruisers flame,

The motor-launches with their searchlights bristle
About the targets. You are black. You shout,
And cup your broken sword-hand. Yes, your whistle
Across the crackling water: *Quick, the ice is out.* . . .
The wind dies in our canvas; we were running dead
Before the wind, but now our sail is part
Of death. O Brother, a New England town is death
And incest—and I saw it whole. I said,
Life is a thing I own. Brother, my heart
Races for sea-room—we are out of breath.

Mother Marie Therese

DROWNED IN 1912

The speaker is a Canadian nun stationed in New Brunswick.

OLD sisters at our Maris Stella House
        Remember how the Mother's strangled grouse
And snow-shoe rabbits matched the royal glint
Of Pio Nono's vestments in the print
That used to face us, while our aching ring
Of stationary rockers saw her bring
Our cake. Often, when sunset hurt the rocks
Off Carthage, and surprised us knitting socks
For victims of the Franco-Prussian War,
Our scandal'd set her frowning at the floor;
And vespers struck like lightning through the gloom
And oaken ennui of her sitting room.
It strikes us now, but cannot re-inspire;
False, false and false, I mutter to my fire.
The good old times, ah yes! But good, that all's
Forgotten like our Province's cabals;
And Jesus, smiling earthward, finds it good;
For we were friends of Cato, not of God.
This sixtieth Christmas, I'm content to pray
For what life's shrinkage leaves from day to day;
And it's a sorrow to recall our young
Raptures for Mother, when her trophies hung,
Fresh in their blood and color, to convince
Even Probationers that Heaven's Prince,
Befriending, whispered: "Is it then so hard?
Tarry a little while, O disregard
Time's wings and armor, when it flutters down
Papal tiaras and the Bourbon crown;
For quickly, priest and prince will stand, their shields
Before each other's faces, in the fields,
Where, as I promised, virtue will compel
Michael and all his angels to repel

Satan's advances, till his forces lie
Beside the Lamb in blissful fealty."
Our Indian summer! Then, our skies could lift,
God willing; but an Indian brought the gift.
"A sword," said Father Turbot, "not a saint";
Yet He who made the Virgin without taint,
Chastised our Mother to the Rule's restraint.
Was it not fated that the sweat of Christ
Would wash the worldly serpent? Christ enticed
Her heart that fluttered, while she whipped her hounds
Into the quicksands of her manor grounds,
A lordly child, her habit fleur-de-lys'd—
There she dismounted, sick; with little heed,
Surrendered. Like Proserpina, who fell
Six months a year from earth to flower in hell;
She half-renounced by Candle, Book and Bell
Her flowers and fowling pieces for the Church.
She never spared the child and spoiled the birch;
And how she'd chide her novices, and pluck
Them by the ears for gabbling in Canuck,
While she was reading Rabelais from her chaise,
Or parroting the *Action Française*.
Her letter from the soi-disant French King,
And the less treasured golden wedding ring
Of her shy Bridegroom, yellow; and the regal
Damascus shot-guns, pegged upon her eagle
Emblems from Hohenzollern standards, rust.
Our world is passing; even she, whose trust
Was in its princes, fed the gluttonous gulls,
That whiten our Atlantic, when like skulls
They drift for sewage with the emerald tide.
Perpetual novenas cannot tide
Us past that drowning. After Mother died,

36

"An émigrée in this world and the next,"
Said Father Turbot, playing with his text.
Where is he? Surely, he is one of those,
Whom Christ and Satan spew! But no one knows
What's happened to that porpoise-bellied priest.
He lodged with us on Louis Neuvième's Feast,
And celebrated her memorial mass.
His bald spot tapestried by colored glass,
Our angels, Prussian blue and flaking red,
He squeaked and stuttered: "N-n-nothing is so d-dead
As a dead s-s-sister." Off Saint Denis' Head,
Our Mother, drowned on an excursion, sleeps.
Her billy goat, or its descendant, keeps
Watch on a headland, and I hear it bawl
Into this sixty-knot Atlantic squall,
"Mamamma's Baby," past Queen Mary's Neck,
The ledge at Carthage—almost to Quebec,
Where Monsieur de Montcalm, on Abraham's
Bosom, asleep, perceives our world that shams
His New World, lost—however it atones
For Wolfe, the Englishman, and Huron bones
And priests'. O Mother, here our snuffling crones
And cretins feared you, but I owe you flowers:
The dead, the sea's dead, has her sorrows, hours
On end to lie tossing to the east, cold,
Without bed-fellows, washed and bored and old,
Bilged by her thoughts, and worked on by the worms,
Until her fossil convent come to terms
With the Atlantic. Mother, there is room
Beyond our harbor. Past its wooden Boom
Now weak and waterlogged, that Frontenac
Once diagrammed, she welters on her back.

The bell-buoy, whom she called the Cardinal,
Dances upon her. If she hears at all,
She only hears it tolling to this shore,
Where our frost-bitten sisters know the roar
Of water, inching, always on the move
For virgins, when they wish the times were love,
And their hysterical hosannahs rouse
The loveless harems of the buck ruffed grouse,
Who drums, untroubled now, beside the sea—
As if he found our stern virginity
Contra naturam. We are ruinous;
God's Providence through time has mastered us:
Now all the bells are tongueless, now we freeze,
A later Advent, pruner of warped trees,
Whistles about our nunnery slabs, and yells,
And water oozes from us into wells;
A new year swells and stirs. Our narrow Bay
Freezes itself and us. We cannot say
Christ even sees us, when the ice floes toss
His statue, made by Hurons, on the cross,
That Father Turbot sank on Mother's mound—
A whirligig! Mother, we must give ground,
Little by little; but it does no good.
Tonight, while I am piling on more driftwood,
And stooping with the poker, you are here,
Telling your beads; and breathing in my ear,
You watch your orphan swording at her fears.
I feel you twitch my shoulder. No one hears
Us mock the sisters, as we used to, years
And years behind us, when we heard the spheres
Whirring *venite;* and we held our ears.
My mother's hollow sockets fill with tears.

David and Bathsheba
in the Public Garden

I

DAVID TO BATHSHEBA

"WORN out of virtue, as the time of year,
The burning City and its bells surround
The Public Garden. What is sound
Past agony is fall:
The children crowding home from school at five,
Punting a football in the bricky air—
You mourn Uriah? If he were alive,
O Love, my age were nothing but the ball
Of leaves inside this lion-fountain, left
For witch and winter." "Yet the leaves' complaint
Is the King's fall . . . whatever suffers theft."
"The Latin labels on the foreign trees are quaint.

The trees, for decades, shook their discontent
On strangers; rustling, rustling the Levant."
"Uriah might have found the want
Of what was never his
A moment, found the falling colors welcome."
"But he was dead before Jehovah sent
Our shadows to the lion's cave. What's come
Is dancing like a leaf for nothing. Kiss:
The leaves are dark and harp." "My Lord, observe
The shedding, park-bound mallards, how they keep
Circling and diving for Uriah's sleep;
Driven, derided, David, and my will a curve.

The fountain's falling waters ring around
The garden." "Love, if you had stayed my hand
Uriah would not understand
The lion's rush, or why
This stone-mouthed fountain laps us like a cat."
"And he is nothing after death but ground,
Anger and anguish, David? When we sat
The nights of summer out, the gravity
Of reaching for the moon. . . . Perhaps it took
Of fall, the Fall?" "Perhaps, I live. I lie
Drinking our likeness from the water. Look:
The Lion's mane and age! Surely, I will not die."

II

BATHSHEBA'S LAMENT IN THE GARDEN

Baring the mares'-nests that the squirrels set
To tangle with the wood-winds of the North,
October blows to wood . . . the fourth
Since David broke our vows
And married Abishag to warm him. Cold!
The pigeons bluer with it, since we met
Beside the lion-fountain, and unrolled
The tackle of our model boats. Our prows
Were sworded as the marlin, and they locked,
Clearing the mallards' grotto, half a mile
Up pond—and foundered; and our splashing mocked
The lion's wrinkled brow. My Love, a little while,

The lion frothed into the basin . . . all,
Water to water—water that begets
A child from water. And the jets
That washed our bodies drowned
The curses of Uriah when he died
For David; still a stranger! *Not-at-all,*
We called him, after the withdrawing tide
Of Joab's armor-bearers slew him, and he found
Jehovah, the whale's belly of the pit.
He is the childless, the unreconciled
Master of darkness. Will Uriah sit
And judge? You nod and babble. But, you are a child;

At last, a child—what we were playing, when
We blew our bubbles at the moon, and fought
Like brothers, and the lion caught
The moonbeams in its jaws.
The harvest moon, earth's friend, that cared so much
For us and cared so little, comes again;
Always a stranger! Farther from my touch,
The mountains of the moon . . . whatever claws
The harp-strings chalks the harper's fingers. Cold
The eyelid drooping on the lion's eye
Of David, child of fortune. I am old;
God is ungirded; open! I must surely die.

The Fat Man in the Mirror

[AFTER WERFEL]

WHAT'S filling up the mirror? O, it is not I;
    Hair-belly like a beaver's house? An old dog's eye?
        The forenoon was blue
        In the mad King's zoo
Nurse was swinging me so high, so high!

The bullies wrestled on the royal bowling green;
Hammers and sickles on their hoods of black sateen. . . .
        Sulking on my swing
        The tobacco King
Sliced apples with a pen-knife for the Queen.

This *I*, who used to mouse about the paraffined preserves,
And jammed a finger in the coffee-grinder, serves
        Time before the mirror.
        But this pursey terror . . .
Nurse, it is a person. *It is nerves.*

Where's the Queen-Mother waltzing like a top to staunch
The blood of Lewis, King of Faerie? Hip and haunch
        Lard the royal grotto;
        Straddling Lewis' motto,
Time, the Turk, its sickle on its paunch.

Nurse, Nurse, it rises on me . . . O, it starts to roll,
My apples, O, are ashes in the meerschaum bowl. . . .
        If you'd only come,
        If you'd only come,
Darling, if . . . The apples that I stole,

While Nurse and I were swinging in the Old One's eye . . .
Only a fat man with his beaver on his eye
>   Only a fat man,
>   Only a fat man
Bursts the mirror. O, it is not I!

Thanksgiving's Over

Thanksgiving night, 1942: a room on Third Avenue. Michael dreams of his wife, a German-American Catholic, who leapt from a window before she died in a sanatorium. The church referred to in the first and last stanzas is the Franciscan church on 31st Street.

THANKSGIVING night: Third Avenue was dead;
My fowl was soupbones. Fathoms overhead,
Snow warred on the El's world in the blank snow.
"Michael," she whispered, "just a year ago,
Even the shoreleave from the *Normandie*
Were weary of Thanksgiving; but they'd stop
And lift their hats. I watched their arctics drop
Below the birdstoup of the Anthony
And Child who guarded our sodality
For lay-Franciscans, Michael, till I heard
The birds inside me, and I knew the Third
Person possessed me, for I was the bird
Of Paradise, the parrot whose absurd
Garblings are glory. *Cherry ripe, ripe, ripe:*
I shrilled to Christ the Sailor's silver pipe
And cherry-tasselled tam. Now Michael sleeps,
Thanksgiving's over, nothing is for keeps:
New earth, new sky, new life: I hear the word
Of Brother Francis, child and bird, descend,
Calling the war of Michael a pretend;
The Lord is Brother Parrot, and a friend."

"Whose friend?" I answered. I was dreaming. Cars
Trampled the Elevated's scaffolding,
And jerked the fire-proofed pumpkins on the line
Her Aunt had fixed with Christophers and stars
To make her joyful; and the bars
Still caged her window—half a foot from mine,
It mirrored mine:
My window's window. On its cushioned ring,
Her celluloid and bargain cockatoo,

Yellow and blue,
Grew restive from her fingering—
Poor numskull, he had beebees in his tail.
"The birds inside me choir to Christ the Healer;
Thanksgiving's over." She was laughing. Bars
Shielded her vigil-candle, while it burned
Pin-beaded, indigo:
A bluebird in a tumbler. "Let me go!
Michael," she whispered, "all I want to do
Is kill you." Then the bars
Crashed with her, and I saw her vanishing
Into the neon of the restaurant—
Clawing and screaming . . . "If you're worth the burying
And burning, Michael, God will let you know
Your merits for the love I felt the want
Of, when your mercy shipped me to Vermont

To the asylum. Michael, was there warrant
For killing love? As if the birds that range
The bestiary-garden by my cell,
Like angels in the needle-point, my Aunt
Bequeathed our altar guild, could want
To hurt a fly! . . . But Michael, I was well;
My mind was well;
I wanted to be loved—to thaw, to change,
To *April!* Now our mountains, seventeen
Bald Brothers, green
Below the timberline, must change
Their skullcaps for the green of Sherwood Forest;
Mount Leather-Jacket leads the season. Outlaws,
We enter a world of children, perched on gaunt
Crows-nests in hemlocks over flat-iron torrents;

And freely serve our term
In prison. I will serve you, Love. Affirm
The promise, move the mountains, while they lean,
As dry as dust for want
Of trusting. Michael, look, the lordly range
Over our brooks' chorale of broken rocks,
Lifting a bowshot's distance, clouds and suffers change—
Blue cloud! There, ruin toils not, though infirm:
Our water-shed! Our golden weathercocks
Are creaking: Fall is here, and starlings. Flocks
Scavenge for El Dorado in the hemlocks.

O Michael, hurry up and ring my bell.
Ring, ring for me! . . . Why do you make us kneel?
Why are we praying? Michael, Venus locks
My lattice, lest a chatterbox
Archangel—O so jealous—spoil and steal
Her commonweal,
My bedroom. Is it just another cell,
This *Primavera*, where the Graces wear
Only the air:
Unmarried April! It is hell!
A lying-in house where the Virtues wither.
I promise, Michael. Michael, I will promise.
I promise on my kneeler—in these stocks!
Your Virtues, owls or parrots, bend my ear
And babble: *Chatterer,*
Our owlet, once in a blue moon we stir;
Our elbows almost touch you. How we care
And worry, Goldielocks;
Thanksgiving's Goose, poor loveless Venus: life's a sell:
Our loveless fingers crook to crunch your sage
And parsley through your wishbone—you! I'll tell

You, Michael Darling: an adulterer,
My Husband, shows me in a parrot's cage
And feeds me like a lion. While I age,

Virtues and elders eye me. Love, the outrage
Would have undone me, if my mind had held
Together, half a moment. Altar boys
Lit candles with my diary. Page by page,
Its refuse, sparkling through my cage,
Branded me, Michael!" Then a popping noise:
It was her toy's
Fragments: her cockatoo. She yelled.
The whisky tumbler in her hand
Became a brand.
Her pigtails that her Aunt had belled
To tell us she was coming, flashed and tinkled.
"Husband, you used to call me Tomcat-kitten;
While we were playing Hamlet on our stage
With curtain rods for foils, my eyes were bleeding;
I was your valentine.
You are a bastard, Michael, aren't you! *Nein*,
Michael. It's no more valentines." Her hand
Covered her eyes to cage
Their burning from the daylight. Sleep dispelled
The burden of her spirit. But the cars
Rattled my window. *Where am I to go?* She yelled:
"Let go my apron!" And I saw them shine,
Her eyeballs—like a lion at the bars
Across my open window—like the stars!

Winter had come on horseback, and the snow,
Hostile and unattended, wrapped my feet

In sheepskins. Where I'd stumbled from the street,
A red cement Saint Francis fed a row
Of toga'd boys with birds beneath a Child.
His candles flamed in tumblers, and He smiled.
"Romans!" she whispered, "look, these overblown
And bootless Brothers tell us we must go
Barefooted through the snow where birds recite:
Come unto us, our burden's light—light, light,
This burden that our marriage turned to stone!
O Michael, must we join this deaf and dumb
Breadline for children? Sit and listen." So
I sat. I counted to ten thousand, wound
My cowhorn beads from Dublin on my thumb,
And ground them. *Miserere?* Not a sound.

DATE DUE

FEB 27 '69			
Covington			
Reserve			
E ng 16			
MAY 14 '69			
GAYLORD			PRINTED IN U.S.A.